Materials

Graham Peacock

Wayland

Titles in the series:

ASTRONOMY • ELECTRICITY • FORCES
GEOLOGY • HEAT • LIGHT • MATERIALS
METEOROLOGY • SOUND • WATER

Editor: Kate Asser
Series Designer: Jan Sterling, Sterling Associates
Book Designer: Joyce Chester
Consultant: Jane Battell, Science Advisory Teacher
Photo stylist: Zoë Hargreaves

First published in 1994 by
Wayland (Publishers) Ltd
61 Western Road, Hove
East Sussex, BN3 1JD, England

British Library Cataloguing in Publication Data

Peacock, Graham
Materials.–(Science Activities Series)
I. Title II. Series
620.1

ISBN 0 7502 0733 7

Acknowledgements
The publishers would like to thank the following for allowing their
pictures to be used in this book: NHPA p9; Science Photo
Library p6, p23.

The publishers would also like to thank the pupils, parents and teachers
of Somerhill Road Junior School, Hove, for their help in making
this book.

Typeset by Dorchester Typesetting Group Ltd
Printed and bound in Italy by G. Canale & C.S.p.A.

Contents

Wood   4

Paper   6

Testing paper   8

Fabrics   10

Plastics   12

Metals   14

Mixing materials   16

Mixtures   18

Solid to liquid   20

Liquids   22

Acids and alkalis   24

Liquid to gas   26

Gases   28

Glossary   30

Books to read   31

Notes for parents and teachers   31

Index   32

Words that appear in **bold** are explained in the glossary
on page 30.

Wood

Wood is a **solid** material. It has a fixed shape and size.

You will need:

♦ **different wooden objects, natural and manufactured**

All the materials we use were either dug out of the earth or came from a living thing. Sometimes these natural materials are used to make other manufactured materials.

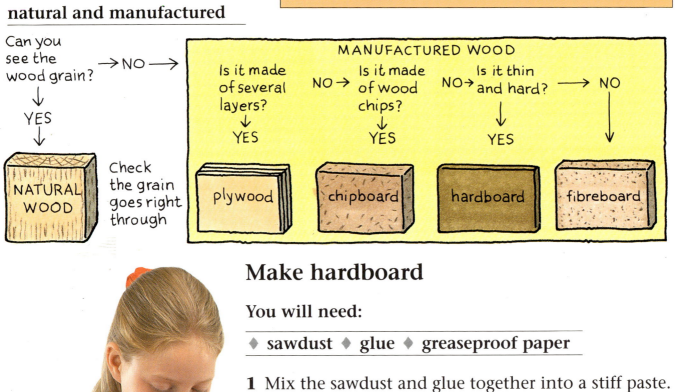

Can you see the wood grain? →NO→

↓
YES
↓

NATURAL WOOD

Check the grain goes right through

MANUFACTURED WOOD

Is it made of several layers? NO→ Is it made of wood chips? NO→ Is it thin and hard? → NO

↓   ↓   ↓   ↓
YES   YES   YES   NO

plywood   chipboard   hardboard   fibreboard

Make hardboard

You will need:

♦ **sawdust** ♦ **glue** ♦ **greaseproof paper**

1 Mix the sawdust and glue together into a stiff paste.

2 Sprinkle sawdust on to a sheet of paper, then spread the paste on top so that it is 5 mm thick.

3 Leave it to set for a day or two.

4 Test the strength of your **hardboard**.

How could you make it stronger?

Good material for a floor?

You will need:

◆ pieces of different materials eg. balsa, hardboard, pine, hardwood ◆ simple tools for tests eg. screwdriver, dropper

1 Think of ways to test the materials to see which would be best for flooring.

2 Carry out your tests. Which material would you use for flooring?

3 Now design a fair test to find the best material for a kitchen cutting board.

You will need an adult's help if you use a knife.

TESTING WOOD FOR A FLOOR

▶ Scratch with a screwdriver
▶ Drop coloured water onto it
▶ Hit with a hammer
▶ Test for strength

2 cm thick

a brick

Floating wood

1 Collect different types of wood. (It is best if they have a similar shape.)

2 Predict which will float the best.

3 Put the pieces of wood into some water. Draw them from the side to show their positions in the water.

Did you know?

Lignum vitae is a wood used to make bowls. It is so **dense** that it sinks in water.

The biggest living thing on earth is the sequoia tree that grows in California, USA. You could make 5,000 million matches from one tree!

Paper

What is paper made from?

You will need:

- ◆ **tissue paper**
- ◆ **newspaper**
- ◆ **sticky tape**
- ◆ **a magnifying glass**
- ◆ **a microscope**

1 Carefully rip a damp sheet of tissue. Look through a magnifying glass at the fibres on the torn edge.

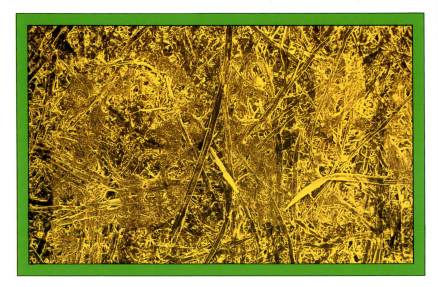

2 Press a piece of sticky tape on to a piece of newspaper. Rip it off. Look at the fibres on the tape through a microscope.

This highly magnified picture of newsprint shows the fibres of wood clearly. Newsprint is made by grinding logs between rough stones.

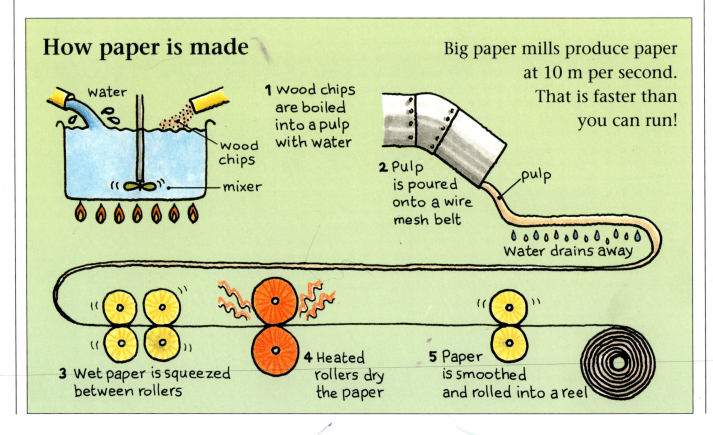

How paper is made

water

1 Wood chips are boiled into a pulp with water

wood chips

mixer

Big paper mills produce paper at 10 m per second. That is faster than you can run!

2 Pulp is poured onto a wire mesh belt

pulp

Water drains away

3 Wet paper is squeezed between rollers

4 Heated rollers dry the paper

5 Paper is smoothed and rolled into a reel

How do you recycle paper?

You will need:

♦ **tissues** ♦ **two thick wads of newspaper** ♦ **a large jug** ♦ **a rolling-pin** ♦ **two sheets of cloth (or clean paper)** ♦ **a sieve**

1 Rip up the tissue paper into shreds.

2 Mix the tissue with plenty of warm water to make a **pulp**.

3 Strain the pulp through the sieve.

4 Spread out the pulp on a piece of cloth or clean paper.

5 Put the other piece of cloth and more newspaper on top. Squeeze out the water using the rolling-pin.

Find out:

● which sort of paper makes the best recycled writing paper

● if it helps to add a little wallpaper to the pulp

Ancient paper

Before paper was invented, people made marks on soft clay tablets.

Chinese people invented the first real paper in AD 105.

Messy ink

Do not use newspaper for your recycling. The ink is very dirty and difficult to clean off your hands.

Testing paper

You will need:

- tissue
- newspaper
- a carrier like the one below
- 2 pencils

1 Carefully rip a sheet of tissue paper in one direction.

2 Now try to rip it in the other direction.

Why do you think that it rips more easily in one direction than in the other?

Find out:

- if newspaper rips more easily one way than the other

Paper strength

1 Cut some paper into the shape shown opposite. Where does it always rip when you pull it?

2 Set up the test for yourself. Which sort of paper is the strongest? Are you sure that your test is fair?

Find out:

- what mass a piece of paper that is 5 mm wide at the neck will hold

- if a piece of paper 10 mm wide at the neck will hold twice as much as one that is 5 mm wide

How strong is a tissue?

You will need:

◆ tissue ◆ a clean, safe tin ◆ a plastic pot (smaller than the tin) ◆ an elastic band ◆ different masses

1 Put a dry tissue over the rim of the can. Hold it in place with an elastic band.

2 Stand the plastic container on the tissue. How much weight will the tissue support?

3 Plan an experiment to find out how much a wet tissue will support.

Make a papier mâché puppet

1 Rip up some newspaper into strips.

2 Soak it in some thin wallpaper paste.

3 Crumple dry newspaper into a ball.

4 Cover the ball with the wet newspaper. Let it dry.

5 Put another layer of strips over the ball. Make a nose and chin from squashed papier mâché.

6 Make a cloak for your puppet.

Natural papier mâché

Some wasps make nests from chewed paper and spit. The paper has coloured layers showing where the wasps have used different woods.

Paper wasps make their nests from chewed-up wood.

9

Fabrics

How are fabrics made?

You will need:

- ♦ different fabrics including nylon tights, felt, wool and printed cotton
- ♦ a magnifying glass or microscope

Sort the **fabrics** into four groups like this:

knitted

felt

Woven and printed

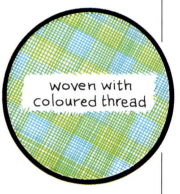
woven with coloured thread

How are threads made?

You will need:

- ♦ a small ball of cotton wool

1 Very gently pull some fibres and twist them with your finger and thumb. (You could try rolling the cotton wool on your knee.)

2 Gently pull and twist until you have twisted a thread.

3 Notice that the twisted thread is much stronger than the loose fibres.

How are fibres dyed?

Warning! You must ask an adult to help with this activity.

You will need:

♦ salt ♦ white or natural wool or white fabric ♦ an old saucepan ♦ a jug
♦ a sieve ♦ fruit or vegetables with colourful juices eg. beetroot, onion skins,
red cabbage, blackberries ♦ 2 bowls

1 Boil the fruit or vegetable for a minute.

2 Remove the pan from the heat. Allow the juice to cool, then strain it into a jug. Throw away the vegetable.

3 Pour the **liquid** into the bowls.

4 Add a spoonful of salt to one of the bowls.

5 Put the undyed wool or fabric into the bowls. Let it soak for a few hours.

6 Take out your dyed fabric or wool and let it dry. Did the salt help the fabric to take in the dye?

Did you know?

The red **dye** cochineal, which is used to colour fabrics, food and lipstick, comes from the boiled and crushed bodies of small insects. The insects live on cacti in South America.

Plastics

You will need:

♦ **strips of plastic (30 cm × 2 cm) from a variety of bags**

1 Gently pull each strip of plastic.

2 What do you notice happening as they begin to stretch?

3 Keep stretching each strip until it is about to snap.

4 Stick all the stretched plastic strips in line on to a piece of paper.

Which carrier bag plastic stretched the most?

Changed plastic

Take the piece of plastic that stretched the most. What do you think will happen if you try to stretch it again?

Is paper as strong as plastic?

To find out, use material from paper and plastic bags in a fair test.

Is plastic or paper best for wall covering?

You will need:

♦ samples of wall coverings, including paper and plastic vinyl ♦ a dropper ♦ oil ♦ sandpaper ♦ water ♦ scissors ♦ kitchen cleaner

1 List some ways to test for the best kitchen wall covering.

2 Carry out your tests and display your results.

3 Which covering would be best in a kitchen? Would you choose it for a bedroom?

Where does it come from?

Most plastic is made from **petroleum**. Plastic is an example of a manufactured material. Make a list of other manufactured materials.

Warm plastic

Plan tests to see if there are differences between warm and cold plastic. Here is an example:

	From the freezer	Room temp	On the radiator
Strip of plastic bag	stretched 14cm	stretched 17cm	stretched 19cm
Blu tack	it feels hard	it feels stretchy	it feels soft

Warning!

Never burn or heat plastic in an oven!

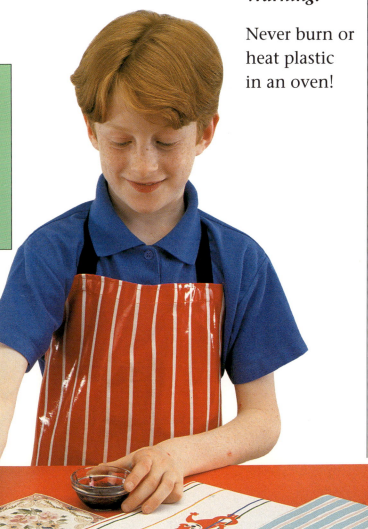

Metals

Are all metals magnetic?

You will need:

♦ different metals, including steel and aluminium ♦ a magnet

Test each metal to see if it is attracted to the magnet.

Did you know?

Cassette tapes are coated with tiny particles of iron. The recording head magnetizes the particles into a code. The playback head reads the code and turns it into electrical signals, which are fed to the loudspeakers.

Are all metals very hard?

You will need:

♦ different clean scrap metal pieces eg. aluminium cans, steel cans, old cutlery, a nail (iron), a screw (steel), a piece of copper pipe

1 Use your nail to scratch the metals.

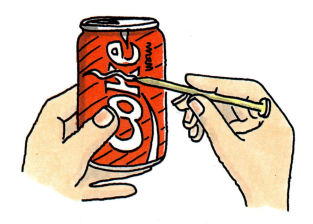

2 How deep does the scratch go into the metal?

3 Put the pieces of metal in order:

softest   hardest

Did you know?

Some metals, like sodium and potassium, are soft enough to be cut with a plastic knife.

Do all metals go rusty?

You will need:

- different scrap metal pieces (include a steel can and an aluminium can – use a magnet to tell the difference)

1 Scratch each object with a screw or nail.

2 Leave the cans and the other metal samples in a damp place for two days. Which go rusty? Where does the steel can go rusty?

Tin can?

Steel cans are coated with tin. Tin will not rust, but it is soft so it is easily scratched off.

Did you know?

Aluminium is a light metal, so it is often used to make aeroplanes. If planes were made of steel or iron, they would be three times as heavy!

Do all metals weigh the same?

You will need:

- samples of different metals

Pick up the pieces of metal. Which ones feel heavy for their size? Which feel light for their size?

A 1 cm cube of aluminium has a mass of 2.7 g.

A block of gold the same size has a mass of 19.3 g.

A 1 cm cube of osmium metal has a mass of 22.5 g.

Mixing materials

Making concrete

You will need:

♦ **500 g cement** ♦ **500 g sand** ♦ **5 or 6 small boxes** ♦ **3 spoons** ♦ **water** ♦ **an old container** ♦ **plastic sheeting**

1 Protect the table with the plastic sheet.

2 Measure out 6 spoons of sand and 6 spoons of cement. Mix them together carefully. Add enough water to make a thick mixture.

3 Pour your mixture into a box.

4 Make other concrete mixtures using different amounts of sand and cement.

5 Leave the bars to dry for a day.

Warning! Try not to touch the cement. Wash any splashes off your hands with clean water and protect your eyes.

Test

Which mixture of concrete and sand gives the strongest bars?

Why do apples go brown?

You will need:

♦ **an apple** ♦ **lemon juice**
♦ **sugar** ♦ **water** ♦ **a plastic bag**

1 Carefully cut a slice off the apple.

2 Leave the slice in the open air for an hour. What changes do you notice?

3 Plan an experiment to see if you can stop apple slices going brown.

You could:

● put the slice in a bag

● squeeze lemon juice on it

● sprinkle sugar on it

Oxidation

Apples go brown because they combine with oxygen in the air.

Hot mixture

You will need:

♦ **plaster of Paris** ♦ **Plasticine**
♦ **a small object like a key or a leaf**

1 Make a mould with the Plasticine.

2 Press an object into the bottom of the mould. Take it out.

3 Mix some plaster of Paris with water until the mixture is like thick cream.

4 Pour the plaster into the mould and leave it for half an hour. Feel the mould as the plaster sets.

Chemical reaction

Plaster of Paris gets hot as it sets. This is because it reacts with the water and releases energy as heat. Design an experiment to see if plaster of Paris will set even if the air cannot reach it to dry it out.

Mixtures

You will need:

♦ **a dry mixture of lentils and beans**
♦ **3 bowls** ♦ **a foil dish** ♦ **a sharp pencil** ♦ **a stopwatch**

1 Time how long it takes to separate the beans and lentils using:

● your right hand

● your left hand

● both hands

2 Push the pencil through the foil dish to make a sieve. Push through just enough to make small holes for the lentils to fall through.

How quickly can you sort the lentil and bean mixture now?

Sieve wholemeal flour

bran is left in sieve

small particles of flour go through

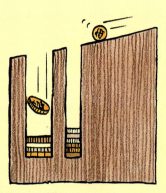

Money sorter

Can you make a money sorter that works like a sieve?

How can you purify rock salt?

You will need:

◆ a small bowl of the salt used on icy roads or a mixture of sand and salt ◆ a filter funnel ◆ filter paper or kitchen towel ◆ warm water

1 To separate the mixture of salt and sand, add water and stir.

What is **dissolved?**

What stays on the bottom?

2 Pour the water through the **filter**.

What gets caught in the paper?

3 Leave the solution of salty water to **evaporate**.

Mastering mixtures

Challenge your friends to separate mixtures of things like:

chips of wax crayon (floats)
tiny staples (magnetic)
sand (not **soluble**)
salt (soluble)
marbles (too big to sieve)
sugar (soluble)

Think of your own mixtures and how to separate them.

Salt production

Salt deposits were laid down millions of years ago. They used to be mined like coal. Most salt is now produced by dissolving the salt under ground.

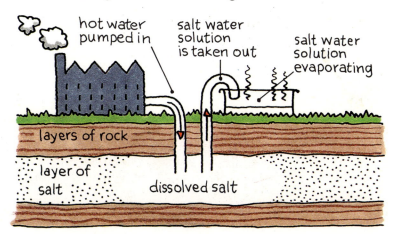

hot water pumped in

salt water solution is taken out

salt water solution evaporating

layers of rock

layer of salt

dissolved salt

Solid to liquid

What changes happen as a candle burns?

Warning! You will need an adult to help you with this activity.

You will need:

♦ **a small candle or night-light standing in a tray of sand**

1 Handle a piece of wax for a few minutes.

   What happens as it warms up in your fingers?

2 Light the candle's wick.

3 What happens when liquid wax runs down the candle?

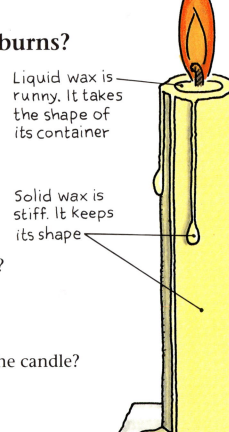

Liquid wax is runny. It takes the shape of its container

Solid wax is stiff. It keeps its shape

Make your own candle

1 Put a short candle into an egg cup or small foil dish.

2 Place a few pieces of broken wax and coloured wax crayon around the candle.

3 Ask an adult to light the candle. Let it burn until all the wax is melted.

4 Blow it out. When it is cool, remove the new candle from its mould.

Watch solids change as flapjacks cook

Warning! Ask for adult help when you are cooking food.

You will need:

- 100 g margarine ◆ 25 g sugar
- 2 tablespoons syrup
- 200 g oats

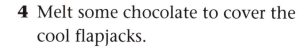

1 With an adult, gently heat the margarine, syrup and sugar in a pan. Watch the two solids become a liquid.

2 Mix the liquid with the oats. Press the mixture into a tin.

3 Cook in the oven at 375° F (190° C or Gas mark 5) for 30 minutes.

4 Melt some chocolate to cover the cool flapjacks.

True or false?

1 The biggest living thing is a . . .
   a) blue whale b) sequoia tree c) mountain

2 Which animals make their nests from chewed wood?
   a) wasps b) bees c) beetles

3 The dye cochineal is made from . . .
   a) crushed conch shells b) insects c) chemicals

4 Which of these is not manufactured?
   a) nylon b) wool c) paint

5 Gold is how many times heavier than aluminium?
   a) twice as heavy b) about five times as heavy
   c) about seven times as heavy

The answers are in this book.

Liquids

Are some liquids runnier than others?

You will need:

♦ water ♦ wallpaper paste ♦ cooking oil ♦ 3 jars with lids ♦ 3 marbles or coins

1 Fill each jar with a different liquid.

Put in the marble or coin and screw on the lid.

2 Turn the jars over, all at the same time. (You will need help.)

Which marble falls the quickest?

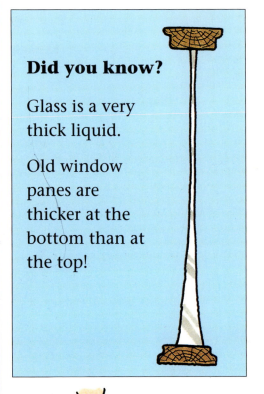

Did you know?

Glass is a very thick liquid.

Old window panes are thicker at the bottom than at the top!

Liquid race

You will need:

♦ different liquids eg. washing-up liquid, liquid cleaner, syrup, water, shampoo, oil ♦ a dropper

Put a drop of each liquid on a tray.

Tilt the tray.

Which liquid runs down most quickly?

(Now wash the tray.)

Are some liquids heavier than others?

You will need:

♦ **cooking oil** ♦ **water** ♦ **coloured salt water** ♦ **a funnel** ♦ **plastic tubing to fit the funnel** ♦ **a clear jar**

1 Pour some water into the jar.

2 Carefully pour the cold salt water underneath the ordinary water, using the tube.

3 Gently pour the oil down the side of the jar, on top of the ordinary water.

4 Leave the jar for a week.

What changes do you notice?

Liquid metal

Mercury is a metal. It is a liquid at room temperature and freezes at -39° C. Mercury is used in thermometers. Its old name was quicksilver.

These shiny drops of the liquid metal Mercury are very poisonous to humans. Mercury is so dense that even iron will float on it.

Acids and alkalis

Can tea be used as an indicator?

Warning! Do not use strong acids or alkalis like bleach for this activity.

You will need:

- ◆ a pot of cool tea ◆ 3 glasses
- ◆ white wine vinegar or lemon juice (acids) ◆ sodium bicarbonate, baking powder or washing powder (alkalis) ◆ 3 teaspoons

1 Pour the cool tea into the glasses.

2 Add two teaspoons of vinegar to one glass. Add one teaspoon of baking powder to another glass.

3 Compare the colours with the tea in the third glass.

Experiment

Do you think you can change the colour of the vinegar and tea mixture by adding small amounts of sodium bicarbonate to it? Try it and see.

pH
When materials dissolve in water, they become **acids** or **alkalis**.
Acidity is measured by pH.

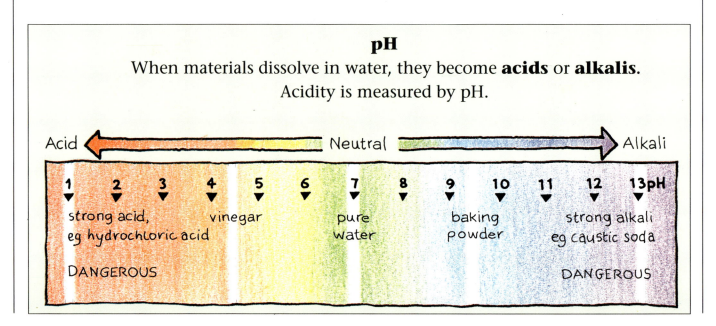

Acid ← Neutral → Alkali

1 2 3 4 5 6 7 8 9 10 11 12 13pH

strong acid, eg hydrochloric acid

vinegar

pure water

baking powder

strong alkali eg caustic soda

DANGEROUS

DANGEROUS

Cabbage colour

You will need:

- ◆ fresh, chopped red cabbage
- ◆ warm water ◆ 2 jugs ◆ a sieve
- ◆ glasses ◆ a variety of safe foods and household cleaners (do not use bleach or lavatory cleaners)

1 Soak the red cabbage in warm water. Squash it with a spoon or masher.

2 Strain the cabbage water into another jug. Pour a little of the water into the glasses.

3 Add drops of vinegar to one glass. Stir a little sodium bicarbonate or washing-up liquid into another. This will show you acid and alkaline colours.

4 Add drops of other substances to clean cabbage water.

5 Make a list of your results.

Indicator paper

The best indicator paper is **universal indicator**.

You can make your own cabbage indicator paper by soaking blotting paper in a strong cabbage **solution**. Let it dry, then cut up the paper. Dip it into different solutions. If the paper goes blue, the solution is an alkali. If it goes red, the solution is an acid.

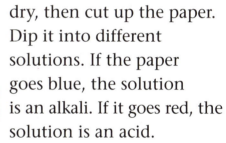

Liquid to gas

Which is the best way to dry washing?

You will need:

♦ **kitchen towel** ♦ **a dropper** ♦ **water**

1 Plan a fair test to find the best way to dry damp paper towels.

2 Check the towels often to see which dries first.

Crisp bread

Plan a test to find out where slices of bread go stale most quickly. Plan another test to discover how best to keep bread fresh.

Container evaporation

Test the idea that water evaporates faster from a bowl than from a bottle.

How will you make the test fair?

Water vapour

When water evaporates, it changes from a liquid to an invisible **gas**.

With an adult, look at a boiling kettle.

Steam evaporates to form invisible water vapour in the air

steam is formed by tiny drops of liquid water

invisible water vapour

DANGER! Steam can badly scald you

Gas to liquid

Why do mirrors and windows steam up?

You will need:

♦ a glass that has been cooled in the fridge ♦ a glass at room temperature

Take the glass out of the fridge. Breathe on it. What do you notice?

Compare it with the warm glass.

Water vapour in your warm breath is cooled when it touches the cold glass. This changes it from a gas to a liquid, which appears as droplets of **condensation**.

Condensation

The water vapour in your breath condenses in cold air.

Gas ➜ liquid ➜ solid

1 Stand a clean, safe can on a plate.

2 Fill it with ice and add lots of salt. Notice the water condensing on the outside of the can.

3 Eventually the ice and salt mixture will become so cold that it **freezes** the condensation on the outside of the can.

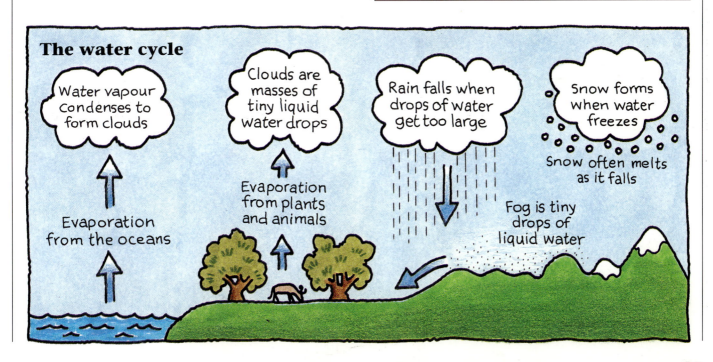

The water cycle

Water vapour condenses to form clouds

Clouds are masses of tiny liquid water drops

Rain falls when drops of water get too large

Snow forms when water freezes

Evaporation from the oceans

Evaporation from plants and animals

Snow often melts as it falls

Fog is tiny drops of liquid water

Gases

How is carbon dioxide produced?

You will need:

♦ a bottle ♦ a balloon
♦ bicarbonate of soda
♦ vinegar

1 Check that the balloon fits over the neck of the bottle.

2 Put half a teaspoon of bicarbonate of soda into the balloon. Pour an egg cupful of vinegar into the bottle.

3 Fix the balloon on to the bottle's neck. Lift up the balloon so that the powder falls into the vinegar.

4 Watch the balloon.

Rising raisins

1 Put a few raisins in a jar with yeast and water. (Do not use 'fast action' yeast.)

2 Can you explain what happens?

Yeast feeds on the sugar in the raisins. It produces the gas **carbon dioxide**.

Fire extinguisher

1 Fix a birthday cake candle in a jar with some Plasticine.

2 Put two teaspoons of bicarbonate of soda into the jar.

3 Light the candle.

4 Dribble some vinegar carefully down the inside of the jar.

5 What happens to the candle?

carbon dioxide gas

Vinegar

dribble in vinegar

candle

jar

Plasticine

bicarbonate of soda

Dissolving gas

Fizzy drinks get their sparkle from carbon dioxide.

1 Empty a fizzy drinks bottle.

2 Quarter-fill it with cold water.

3 Shake the bottle.

4 Explain what happens.

How could you test to see if the effect was really due to the remaining carbon dioxide?

Shrinking air

Put an empty plastic drinks bottle in the fridge or freezer. Predict whether the plastic bottle will get larger or smaller in the cold.

What do you think will happen when it warms up again?

Gases in the atmosphere

Oxygen (21 per cent)

Argon (1 per cent)

Other non-reactive gases

Nitrogen (78 per cent)

Did you know?

Only 0.03 per cent of the air is made up of carbon dioxide.

Harmful UV light absorbed high in the stratosphere by the gas ozone

Ultra violet light

Ozone

By day plants photosynthesise. They take in carbon dioxide and give off oxygen

O_2

CO_2

Animals always take in oxygen and give off carbon dioxide

CO_2

O_2

At night plants respire. They take in oxygen and give off carbon dioxide

CO_2

O_2

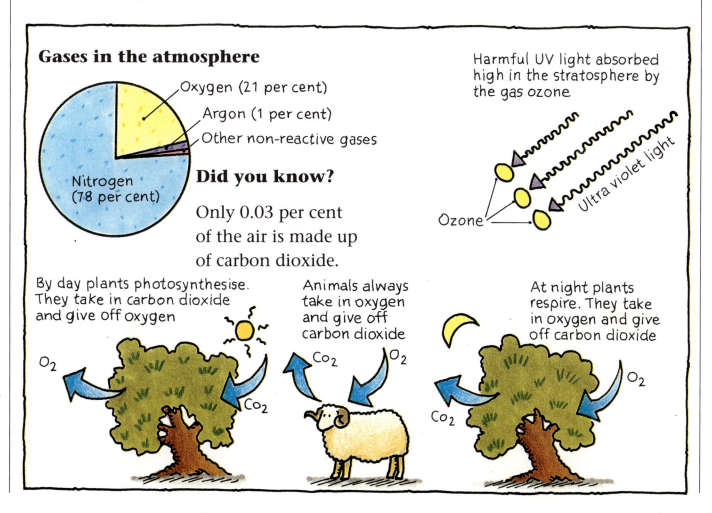

Glossary

Acids Solutions with many free hydrogen particles.

Alkalis Solutions with many free hydroxide particles (a mixture of hydrogen and oxygen).

Carbon dioxide A gas made when particles of carbon join with two atoms of oxygen. Carbon dioxide makes up only a tiny part of the air.

Condensation Droplets of a liquid which has changed from a gas.

Dense Having very tightly packed particles.

Dissolved When particles of a solid have become evenly spaced out in a liquid.

Dye A substance which colours other materials.

Evaporate To change from a liquid to a gas.

Fabrics Materials made from woven, knitted or pressed fibres.

Filter A device for separating mixtures.

Freezes Changes from a liquid to a solid.

Gas A material, like air, which spreads out to fill any container, and has no fixed size or shape.

Hardboard Sheets of hard material made from wood dust and resin squashed together under great pressure.

Indicator A material which shows whether a solution is acid or alkaline.

Lignum vitae A very dense tropical hardwood.

Liquid A material, like water, which flows and takes the shape of a container, but has a fixed size.

Oxidation When a material combines with the gas oxygen. Rust is oxidized iron.

Papier mâché A mixture of ripped-up paper and glue.

Petroleum One of the products made when crude oil is refined.

pH The measure of acidity of a solution, or how many free hydrogen particles it contains.

Pulp A mixture of wood fibres and water.

Solid A material which is stiff and has a fixed size and shape.

Soluble Able to dissolve in a liquid.

Solution A mixture of a solid and liquid in which the molecules of the solid are evenly spaced out. If a solid is dissolved, it will never settle out of the solution unless some of the liquid evaporates.

Universal indicator An indicator which measures the strength of an acid or alkali.

Vinyl A type of plastic often made into sheets for wall and floor covering.

Water vapour Water that has evaporated to become a gas.

Books to read

Pocket Book of Science by Robin Kerrod (Kingfisher, 1990)
101 Science Tricks by Roy Richards (Simon & Schuster, 1990)
100 Simple Science Experiments by Barbara Taylor (Kingfisher, 1990)
Nuffield Primary Science: Materials (Harper Collins, 1993)
The Super Science Book of Materials by Graham Peacock and Cally Chambers (Wayland, 1993)
Wood and Paper (Ginn, 1990)

Notes for parents and teachers

Pages 4-5 The tests for flooring need to be planned before they are carried out.

The way in which the blocks of wood float depends on the density of the wood. Balsa has a very low density and will float high on the water. Whether the blocks float flat on a face or diagonally on a corner depends on the centre of gravity of the block.

Pages 6-7 Commercial paper recyclers use special processes to remove the ink from newsprint and much poor quality recycled paper is used to produce grey board.

Let the children devise their own test on the recycled paper. If they are short of ideas, look at the degree to which ink soaks into their recycled paper.

Pages 8-9 The fibres in most tissue paper are strongly aligned, which gives the paper a grain in one direction. The strength of a piece of paper depends on its width. Twice the width gives twice the strength and so on – the length of the sample is largely irrelevant. Paper is surprisingly strong, so make the samples as narrow as is possible.

Pages 10-11 The cotton wool is very weak before the fibres are twisted together. Friction is the force which stops the fibres sliding past each other and makes the thread strong.

Pages 12-13 Another interesting plastic to test is the packaging that holds groups of cans together. It forms a neck fairly easily and continues to stretch under a relatively small force. Once the plastic has been stretched, it has little strength and the neck will snap very easily.

Pages 14-15 The only magnetic metals you are likely to encounter are iron and steel. Aluminium is much softer than steel.

When kept damp, iron and steel will both rust. Copper will develop a green coating called verdigris, the chemical name for which is copper carbonate.

Pages 16-17 Concrete is not especially dangerous, but it can irritate the skin of some people. Remind the children to wear an apron to protect their clothing. Other materials which oxidize include potatoes and wine.

Pages 18-19 If you find it difficult to obtain rock salt, simply mix the sand and salt together. When filtering, use a coffee filter if this is more convenient than a funnel and paper cone.

Pages 20-21 Always clear the table when working with candles. Tie back loose hair and clothing. Never leave young children alone with candles and matches.

When making your own candle, notice that the liquid wax takes the shape of its container.

Pages 22-23 The thickness of liquids is measured by viscosity. Liquids become less viscous as they warm up. You could put identical blobs of liquid on two trays and compare them after one had been in the fridge for an hour and one left at room temperature.

Pages 24-25 The concept of acids and alkalis is a difficult one for children to grasp, so allow them to explore the effects and colour changes rather than worrying about the underlying chemistry. An acid will neutralize an alkali and vice versa.

Pages 26-27 When looking at the condensation on the outside of a cold can, many children believe that in some way it comes from inside the can. The cold, empty glass provides a starting point for helpful discussion.

When you open the freezer door, you will often see water vapour from the air condense into a cloud of tiny droplets as it is suddenly cooled by the air from the freezer.

Pages 28-29 The raisins bob up and down in the jar as they are buoyed up by the carbon dioxide gas, then fall back to the bottom when the gas bubbles float away. Carbon dioxide is highly soluble, so the fizzy drinks bottle collapses as the gas is dissolved. If you drink the water after shaking the bottle, it tastes like flat soda water.

Index

acids 24-5, 30
aeroplanes 15
alkalis 24-5, 30
aluminium 15
ancient Egyptians 7

candles 20
carbon dioxide 28-9, 30
Chinese 7
cochineal 11
concrete 16
condensation 27, 30
cooking 21
cooling of gases 29

dye 11, 30

evaporation 19, 26, 30

fabrics 10-11, 30
fibres 6, 10
filters 19
fizzy drinks 29
freezing 27, 30

gases 28, 30
glass 22
gold 15

hardboard 4-5, 30

indicators 24-5, 30

lignum vitae 5, 30
liquids 20, 22, 30

man-made materials 4
melting solids 21
mercury 23
metal 14-15, 23
mixtures 16-17, 18-19

newspaper 6, 8

osmium 15
oxidation 17, 30

paper 6-7, 8-9
paper wasps 9
papier mâché 9, 30
pH 24, 30
plaster of Paris 17
plastic 12-13
pulp 7, 30
purification 17

recycling paper 7

rock salt 19
rusting 15

salt production 19
separating mixtures 18-19
sequoia tree 5
solids 4-5, 26, 30
solutions 19, 30
steam 26
strength of
    cement 16
    paper 8-9
    plastic 12

testing
    paper 8-9
    plastic 12-13
threads 10
tissue 6, 8

universal indicator 25, 30
vegetable dye 11

wax 20
water 19, 26-7
    cycle 27
    vapour 26-7, 30
wholemeal flour 18
wood 4-5